The typography idea book

KU-589-116

Inspiration from 50 masters

Alex Steinweiss / Andrew Bryom / Saul Bass / Mehmet Ali Türkmen / Dave Towers / Brian Lightbody / Alvin Lustig / Alan Fletcher / Paula Scher / Kevin Cantrell / Robert Massin / Herb Lubalin / OCD / Alan Kitching / Elvio Gervasi / Francesco Cangiullo / Priest+Grace / Fiodor Sumkin / Alejandro Paul / Zuzana Licko / Jonny Hannah / Jon Gray / A.M. Cassandre / Seymour Chwast / Paul Cox / Nicklaus Troxler / Sascha Hass / Ben Barry / Michiel Schuurman / Paul Sych / Zsuzsanna Ilijin / Stephen Doyle / El Lissitzky / Wim Crouwel / Experimental Jetset / Wing Lau / Josef Müller-Brockmann / Herbert Bayer / Áron Jancsó / Jamie Reid / Tom Carnase / Milton Glaser / Rizon Parein / Roger Excoffon / Paul Belford / Alexander Vasin / Lester Beall / Neville Brody / Eric Gill / Tom Eckersley

Steven Heller and Gail Anderson

Laurence King Publishing

Contents

Introduction:
Make great typography

——————————— Not every designer is a good, much less a great, typographer. Actually, to be a great typographer you have to be a highly skilled graphic designer in the first place. Typography is, arguably, the most important component of graphic design. It requires a distinct ability to make readable messages while expressing, emoting and projecting concepts to audiences, large and small.

Typography can be copied and, therefore, it can be taught. Like the classical painting student learning to perfect the rendering of human form by repeatedly drawing from the same plaster cast, the best way to learn typography is to do it over and over again. Theory is fine, but practice is necessary in order to develop a visceral feeling about the way letters sit on a page or screen. You must know if they are in harmony, or unsuited to marriage. Playing with typographic puzzle pieces is one of the joys of typography. While the end result must be understandable – though please note that doesn't necessarily mean legible, for illegibility is relative and what is illegible can often be deciphered – the process can be intuitive. What you see is more than what you get: playing with type is an opportunity to create typographic personalities both for yourself and for your clients.

This book is geared towards helping you evolve different typographic characters or styles, or perhaps even your specific design signature. What this book is *not* is a tutorial in typographic basics – kerning, spacing, selecting, and so on. There are many excellent existing volumes that will give you that essential knowledge. Our intention here is to lay out many of the fun, esoteric and eccentric options a typographer has at his or her disposal. These 'commonly uncommon' approaches include type transformation and mutation, as well as puns and metaphors, and typographic pastiche and quotation.

In other words if typographic basics are the 'main course' in your typographic feeding frenzy, the ideas herein are the dessert. It's time to indulge yourself in what is offered on the menu of typographic confections.

Communicate through letters

Alex Steinweiss / Andrew Bryom / Saul Bass / Mehmet Ali Türkmen / Dave Towers / Brian Lightbody

Pictorial
Image as letter/symbol

They say that a picture is worth a thousand words, so, what if that picture is of a letter or word? Then it must be worth even more. What we call pictorial type may not be pure typography, but it can be effective design.

Alex Steinweiss's 1941 cover design for *AD* (Art Director) magazine is a pictorial–letter combo. The theme of this issue was the aesthetics of recorded music, including a written profile about Steinweiss, America's album-design pioneer, who was the first designer to use original art on a record sleeve, in this instance for Columbia Records. When asked to design a custom nameplate for the publication, for semiotic reasons Steinweiss (1917–2011) used a draftsman's set-square, or triangle, as the A to represent design, and a semi-circle, or half a 78 rpm record, as the D. It clearly reads as AD, but it also symbolizes record design.

Employing an illustrative conceit such as this is practical only when the image is in conceptual harmony with the content being illustrated. In the case of *AD,* Steinweiss made a flawless connection. Just a year or two before, however, the same magazine was called *PM* (Production Manager) – one wonders which images he might have used then to represent those letters and whether he would have struggled to establish a personal connection with them? Timing is everything.

Making this pictorial technique work may seem as easy as fitting a square peg into a square hole, but the trick to making *great* illustrative typography is in not forcing the wrong image into that hole.

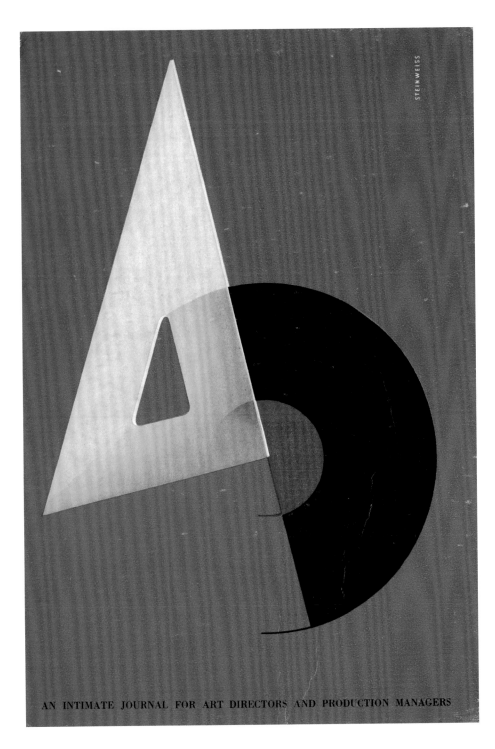

AN INTIMATE JOURNAL FOR ART DIRECTORS AND PRODUCTION MANAGERS

Communicate through letters

⊠ Alex Steinweiss, 1941
AD magazine

⊠ Andrew Byrom, 2001
Interior and Interior Light

Environmental
Alphabet as monument

Some alphabets designed for site-specific environments convey clear messages to passers-by, yet others are designed solely as environmental spectaculars, in which the ironic use of scale and surprising materials is the only rationale for the existence of the work. These 'spectaculars' should be considered as artworks that use letters, rather than as typographic megaphones sending out overt promotional or political messages.

British-born Andrew Byrom, who has produced grand-scale typography for the purposes of both art and design, cleverly made the typeface Interiors from tubular steel usually used for furniture. The typeface is complemented by his wittily conceived Interiors Light, which is the same typographic family structure but made from neon lighting tubes. Both were made for spectacle.

Byrom sees type everywhere and in virtually everything. Interiors started, nevertheless, as a two-dimensional alphabet made by pasting shapes into Adobe Illustrator and, later, into Fontographer. The final letters became full-scale furniture frames, which were ultimately constructed in 3-D using tubular steel. 'Because the underlying design concept is typographical, the end result becomes almost freestyle furniture design,' Byrom explains. 'Letters like m, n, o, b and h can be viewed as simple tables and chairs, but other letters, like e, g, a, s, t, v, x and z, become – when viewed as furniture – more abstract.'

Interiors is not an unprecedented typeface in terms of the letter shapes but, with it, Byrom succeeded in producing both a traditional typeface and a monumental work of art.

Construction
Building a scene with type

The titles on classic blockbuster-movie posters for films such as *Ben Hur*, *El Cid* and *King of Kings* look as if they were carved out of stone. These are metaphorical constructions for historical subjects, but there are more contemporary ways of achieving this kind of dual purpose, in which type is also used to represent an aspect of a narrative: Saul Bass's poster for *Grand Prix* succeeds in announcing the name of the film while illustrating the race track around which this action movie is centred. By adding speed lines to the bold gothic title on the speedway, Bass immediately telegraphs salient plot points and shows the thrust of the plotline.

Practically, this type treatment can be used at many sizes, including extremely large for posters and relatively small for spot newspaper advertisements. The choice of black as the only type colour forces us to see the poster as a totality, not separate headline and illustration.

Bass's typography demonstrates the power of a fully integrated image. Expressive ideas like this do not have to be strained or clichéd, but can be simple, modern and pleasing to the eye.

Making a seamless typographic illustration in this manner will serve as a metaphorical shorthand and place your poster or book jacket firmly in time and place.

⊠ Saul Bass, 1966
Grand Prix

A JOHN FRANKENHEIMER FILM IN CINERAMA

GRAND PRIX

STARRING
JAMES GARNER·EVA MARIE SAINT·YVES MONTAND
TOSHIRO MIFUNE·BRIAN BEDFORD·JESSICA WALTERS
ANTONIO SABATO·FRANCOISE HARDY·ADOLFO CELI

Directed by John Frankenheimer · Produced by Edward Lewis

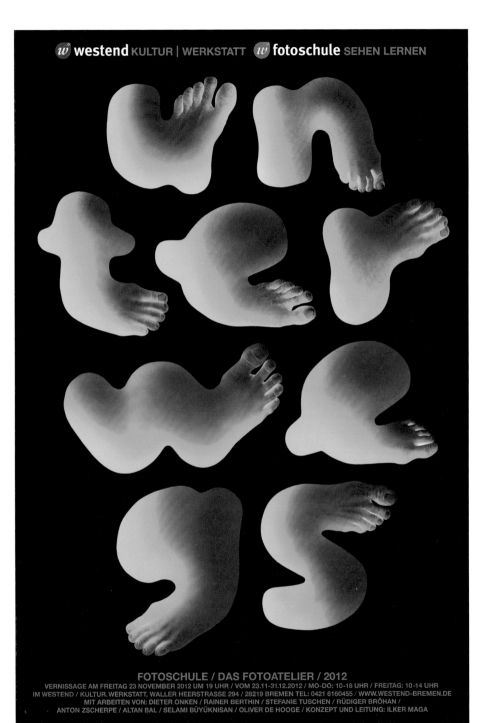

Transformative
Alphabetical feet

──────────── **Today, type can be made from a foot, a hand or just about any other natural, man-made or fantastical object that seems somehow ripe for transformation. These are not real typefaces, of course, nor are they novelty faces (see page 108), which are actually produced in metal, film or digitally, to be used over time. Rather, transformative type is *faux* lettering, created on a whim or for a specific conceptual purpose.**

Turkish designer Mehmet Ali Türkmen created an idiosyncratic alphabet using the feet of his wife and daughter to spell out the title of the poster 'Unterwegs' ('On the Way') for an exhibition at Westend Cultural Centre's Photography School, Bremen. Why a foot? Türkmen explains that it is because a foot represents movement 'in this fast-flowing life' and thus, typographically, interprets the title. He also wanted the poster to caution people to slow down and notice details that remain unseen when they move too fast.

Don't look for objects or body parts turned into letters in any standard type specimen or 'how-to' manual. They will only be found in that veritable Twilight Zone of typographic absurdity, the world of alternative types. But poor quality is never acceptable, even in this unregulated world. Talent and skill are required to transform non-alphabetical shapes into something typographical that is both legible and readable.

☒ Mehmet Ali Türkmen, 2012
Fotoschule/Das Fotoatelier,
'Unterwegs'

Conceptual
Out-of-body type experience

The conventional way to compose editorial text is to arrange columns vertically on a simple grid, either flush left or justified, so that one text block leads into the next. The majority of books, magazines and newspapers adhere to this convention and it is the most expected and navigable way to read consecutive lines and paragraphs. It is not, however, the only way to set type and lay out an editorial page.

Our brains are flexible enough to navigate more contorted typographical highways, as long as there are no impassable detours along the way. That's what English designer Dave Towers has accomplished with his eight-page layout for an interview with film director Tony Kaye. Although he erects a few detours, the ride is bump-free, exciting reading.

Towers's conceptually audacious typography involves reworking columns of the question/answer format into a body text–headline combo that is both the title ('Tony Kaye') *and* the editorial content. Although there may have been an element of serendipity, it required a modicum of pre-planning to make the text fit and remain readable across the two words. A few columns are moderately skewed and some are more jarringly off-kilter, requiring a little more effort on the part of the reader. The reader must also get used to the wide lines of text that form the letters Y and O. And also accept that Towers had to cheat, albeit elegantly, with the crossbars of the A.

The columns of text were Towers's response to reading an unedited word-for-word script of the recorded conversation. The conversation rolls from one subject straight into another, quite unrelated, topic without paragraph breaks, almost in a stream of consciousness.

This is not everyday typography and not every editor would have had the foresight to see that the reader would be drawn into the unusual form. But Towers took on the challenge and created the kind of spreads that show typography is not simply governed by rules and regulations, but by guts and gumption.

⊠ Dave Towers, 2013
'Tony Kaye'

Comic
Serious design

Comic type is not to be mistaken for Comic Sans, a typeface that is as widely overused as it is savagely ridiculed. Comic type is playful, sometimes in its form, but equally often in its application. A seemingly lighthearted take on a challenging subject can have greater impact than a more serious approach, allowing the audience to look at a problem in a less formal way. Humour can often be the best way to get in through the back door.

Writer Julie Rutigliano teamed up with designer Brian Lightbody to create a newspaper campaign for Rock the Vote, a non-partisan organization that seeks to build political power for young people in the United States. The goal for the ads was clear, according to Rutigliano: 'We wanted to get people off their couches and into the polls for the 2008 presidential election.' Their full-page ad, using *The Wall Street Journal*'s Stock Market Index page design creates a powerful commentary on the state of the US economy prior to the election. Typographic wit is employed to reveal key issues that the country faced, and Rutigliano and Lightbody depict the stock market crashing to the bottom of the newspaper page.

Graphic wit is – or should be – a staple of the design process, a first resort, even if the end result is not humorous. Typography is often described as a playful act – a puzzle-solving activity – and the more instinctual play there is, the more unexpected the design will be. This advertisement is seriously funny and captures people's imagination.

⊠ Julie Rutigliano and
Brian Lightbody, 2008
'Rock the Vote'

Communicate through letters

Create typographic personalities

Alvin Lustig / Alan Fletcher / Paula Scher / Kevin Cantrell / Robert Massin / Herb Lubalin / OCD

Collage
Something borrowed, something new

You may ask whether or not there is a significant difference between collage and ransom-note typography. And, although you would be right to question it, the answer is: yes, there is. The latter (see page 100) is a stylistic signifier for punk and repeats the somewhat overly familiar kidnapper's trope of making 'movie-prop' ransom demands while ensuring their anonymity. Collage, however, is rooted less in movie kitsch and more in the modernist aesthetic that was common in Cubist, Futurist and Dadaist art – with the occasional Surrealist ingredient thrown in too.

Collage involves cutting and pasting (by hand or with digital tools) previously printed material, which could be either old or new typefaces and letters, into a legible typographic composition. It is not recommended for most assignments, but, as Alvin Lustig's book jacket demonstrates, it can complement other type elements nicely.

The 'Gatsby' ransom-note part of the title works seamlessly with the more formal elements. It is also a pleasing alternative to the covers and jackets typically designed for *The Great Gatsby*, which are illustrated with art deco stylizations. This cover is unique both for focusing on the elegant dollar sign and for its modest headline and byline combination.

The skewed, pasted 'Gatsby' letters add a comical quality that plays well against the unpretentious simplicity of the lower-case 'the great' and the downplayed byline. This jacket is typical of Lustig's work in its limited colour palette and type selection. The process of collage gives these capital letters the appearance of typographic variety, though they are in the same Futura type as the other letters, and serves as one of two visual triggers (the other is the dollar sign) that merge into one striking visual.

☒ Alvin Lustig, 1945
The Great Gatsby

WALLPAPER

Re-forming
Tearing and sampling

Here is an exercise that will strengthen your type skills: select ten of your favourite typefaces from existing magazines, newspapers, books, etc.; tear them out of their original contexts, some with and some without coloured or textured backgrounds; finally, recompose the type as new words, with an eye to creating both harmonic and dissonant juxtapositions. You may end up with a Dadaesque concoction or something much more refined. Whatever the outcome, this is one enlightening way to experience the connections and distinctions between typographic styles.

During the 1950s and '60s, designers photographed layers of torn billboards to show how, over time, decay alters type and images, and changes meanings. For some, this proved an inspiration for how to deliberately mutate typefaces for graphic effect. Others saw it as it was: a vernacular form of typographic poetry.

Former UK Pentagram partner, Alan Fletcher, who spent a lifetime engaged in typographic experimentation, used a torn-letter technique – which today is called appropriating or sampling – for making typeface collages that expressed the interconnection between type and type, type and language, and type and media. His cut-up printed letters, taken from mass-media publications, expressed a fascination with the fluidity of language and with the physical ways in which type can accentuate and neutralize words.

Tearing typefaces from their original contexts and recycling them is also a technique used in ransom notes (see page 100) and collage (see page 24), but re-formation is more about pushing the limits artistically through distorting, decaying and distressing.

⊠ Alan Fletcher, 2007
Wallpaper magazine

Obsessive
Eccentricity vs excess

Hand-lettering is increasingly integrated into all forms of art these days because the boundaries separating applied from fine art are continually blurring. Painters, sculptors and even performance artists freely take creative nourishment from graphic design and, likewise, graphic designers and typographers are now being offered places in the art world to hang their art, where once they were shunned.

Paula Scher's expressive hand-lettering, inspired by the primitive painter Howard Finster, started as a new approach to solving her illustration and design problems and evolved into paintings and prints that are embraced by the art world. Her rough-hewn hand-painted lettering is the core of a conceptual series of comically skewed maps on canvas, which are tightly packed with the names of every city, province, town, river and ocean in a particular geographical area. Scher calls these maps 'opinionated, biased, erroneous, and, also, sort of right'. The details that fill the paintings are unfailingly seductive – the fruitful product of an obsessive mind.

What's more, though we are now in an age of data visualization in which zealously composed graphic information equals *gravitas*, Scher's maps are not for real-information consumers. Their satiric, almost sarcastic, relationship to information graphics smashes cartographic norms and also reflects a growing trend in typographic density.

The challenge, if one is interested in developing this genre of presenting info, or what Scher calls '*faux* info', is to understand, as she does, the difference between typographic eccentricity and typographic excess. In other words, obsession has its limitations: it is okay to be non-conformist, just not crazy.

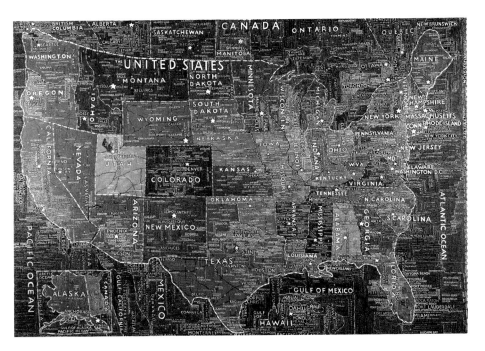

⊠ Paula Scher, 2007
United States

⊠ Kevin Cantrell, 2014
'Terra'

Extreme
More is more

Filling up typographic space with ornament is no more a mistake than extreme reduction is a virtue. Effective typography depends on what goes into or comes out of the space.

Understanding the nature of the assignment and the ultimate use that the typography will have, is all the justification for embellishment that is necessary. But not all designers agree...

Modernists believed that ornament was absurd; it sullied both the aesthetic and the content of design. Adherents of the slightly earlier Arts and Crafts movement, however, believed that ornament should be produced by the skill and handcraft of humans rather than from the templates of machines. Both approaches work in eclectic contemporary design, and even admirers of minimalist typography have to appreciate the extreme intricacy of American designer and art director Kevin Cantrell's virtually illegible, but nonetheless passionately compulsive, Terra type specimen, engraved in wood using lasers by the printer Big Secret.

The awesome detailing is to be admired but not necessarily mimicked. To use this as a model demands the designer understand Cantrell's stunning balance of elements. A good typographer must avoid the understandably insatiable urge to be a typographic gourmand. Extreme typographic display is tasty, but it is also easy to consume more ornament than the eye can truly digest. Appreciate Cantrell's facility in making a complex typographic image, but be wary about introducing it where it is not welcome.

Talking
Speech made visual

Parole in libertà (words in freedom) is the poetic term that Italian Futurists applied to 'noisy' typography. Their type didn't actually make audible sounds, of course, but, when read aloud, the combination of letters and words conjured the tenor and timbre of such aural icons as the motor car, aeroplane engines, guns firing and bombs exploding. Unlike figurative or metaphorical typography, these type compositions did not try to imitate the look of anything, such as rain or a mouse's tail, but rather provided the reader with the stimulus to read aloud in order to absorb the entire multi-sensory experience.

Talking type takes its cue from the traditional comic book, where balloons convey dialogue and splash panels convey sounds such as 'WHAM!', 'BOOM!' and 'SMACK!'. This, in part, was Robert Massin's intention when he designed the book based on the script of Eugène Ionesco's *The Bald Soprano*, an absurdist theatrical play about three couples engaged in conversation that descends into the chaos of complete non-sequiturs, flung back and forth. For the text, Massin used different typefaces to represent each actor's voice. As the conversations become more absurdly boisterous, the type size modulates as well; and, as the individual voices criss-cross and overlap, the typeset words smash into and conceal one another. As the characters in the play fight with each other, the text takes on a more 'obstreperous' appearance.

Massin undertook arduous technical feats (including printing type on to rubber and then stretching it) to make his type talk, but the computer has made creating 'words in freedom' much less tedious. Talking type is one of the ways in which typography challenges many senses at once — and it's a popular one. It can be deployed in an all-encompassing way or more subtly, to emphasize certain words through scale, style and changes in proportion.

⊠ Robert Massin, 1964
The Bald Soprano

ouvrir tout grand la bouche

ah ! oh ! oh ! oh ! **allons** de dents
laissez-moi grincer **caïman** Ulysse

je n'en vais habiter ma
cagn dans, m cacao !
les cacaoyers, des cacaoyers donnent pas des cacahuètes donnent du cacao !
les cacaoyers des cacaoyers donnent pas des cacahuètes donnent du cacao !
les cacaoyers cacaoyers **cacaoyers**

Create typographic personalities

THE COOPER UNION SCHOOL OF ART & ARCHITECTURE

Overlapping
A voice for type

Before the rise of digital technology, overlapping or touching letters required a tedious amount of cutting, pasting, photographing and engraving. Few designers had the patience. Yet in the early '60s there was a pioneer of photo-based typography, New York designer Herb Lubalin, who made tightly spaced and overlapping display compositions for ads and magazines that launched a popular style of expressive typography.

Lubalin made letters overlap and interconnect, producing typography that linked words in headlines in a single visual statement – call it a voice with personality. The result was a demonstrative and expressive headline that spoke to the viewer, rather than the usual simple, orderly lines of type. It was a tedious process then, but using today's digital programs, creating Lubalinesque typographic 'oratory' is achievable in less time and with more variations. Although the style has gone in and out of fashion since the 1970s, when executed with nuance and intelligence, overlapping and smashing will always have a place in the typographer's toolkit, to sharpen the reader's focus on the message.

Be warned, however: too much overlapping, touching and smashing will quickly become a tired conceit. And the paradigm represents a 1970s method. So use the style advisedly and do not try to replicate specific work by the master, Herb Lubalin. Just consider how he accomplished what he did.

⊠ Herb Lubalin, 1975
The Cooper Union School
of Art and Architecture

Non-Traditional
Concept-driven typography

Given the time and labour involved, anyone who aspires to design an entire typeface must be passionate about the process as well as the concept. An 'aspirational' typeface is one that is conceptual and emerges out of that passion, and this is especially true of non-traditional fonts. While not all typefaces created in this way are pixel-perfect, creating a conceptual font can result in various happy surprises.

Free, a face that was developed by New York-based firm OCD (The Original Champions of Design), began when the firm was invited to produce a poster that somehow branded and defined their design philosophy for an exhibition.

OCD's Jennifer Kinon and Bobby Martin responded by imagining that the work was for their 'dream client' – the United States of America. According to their imagined brief, this entailed creating a new American flag that was 'about commerce'. From that starting-point came a glowing neon, red, white and blue image spelling out the word 'Free'. This image would represent freedom, capitalism, commercialism, accessibility, open source and more. After lengthy exploration and many iterations, the stars and stripes were replaced by the word 'Free' in angular letters built on grid proportions derived from the original American flag (opposite, bottom left).

Ultimately, and perhaps surprisingly, the angular letters became a lasting viable entity: they were further refined, digitized and made into a useable font. There are already a significant number of typefaces in the world, but non-traditional yet functional approaches still have a place and even a market for designers who are thrilled by the forms.

Create typographic personalities

Small business owners are the new American revolutionaries. Willing to lay down our lives, our fortunes and our honor * we strike out for freedom. We lead a movement toward a stronger, more stable union that functions on a more human-scale. All heart and guts and grit, we find a way to do what we love, our way, every day.

* Excerpt from Presidential remarks July 4 2013

Image of the Studio:
A Portrait of New York City
Graphic Design

41 Cooper Gallery,
Cooper Union
October 1–26, 2013

Design: OCD

OCD, 2013
Free

Be inspired by history

Alan Kitching / Elvio Gervasi / Francesco Cangiullo / Priest+Grace /
Fiodor Sumkin / Alejandro Paul / Zuzana Licko

Antique
Making aesthetic decisions

———————————— **Using antique letters as contemporary typography is incredibly satisfying when the harmony, or indeed dissonance, succeeds. Designers often revel in the tactility of vintage metal or wood type materials, and the act of working with type is not as disassociated from the physical process of composition as working on a computer is. Using antique materials does, nonetheless, demand tapping into a reservoir of aesthetic resources. Just because a typeface or font looks and feels good, it does not automatically ensure an incredible typographic result: it takes all your aesthetic and intuitive know-how.**

Alan Kitching, an English typographer and experimental letterpress artist, uses his huge store of vintage letters to transcend time and style. *Baseline* magazine (for whom he designed and produced this cover typography) states that Kitching has 'a bewildering array of cutting-edge printing technology of the sixteenth, seventeenth, eighteenth and nineteenth centuries', and describes his third-floor studio in a Victorian building in London's Kennington as having 'an ink-drenched atmosphere strikingly unlike the normal environments in which most designers work'. In his typographic time-machine, Kitching engages with printing materials of the past, including letterpress and wood type, to produce genuinely individualistic contemporary graphics.

Although many of the traits of this *Baseline* cover were also discernible 150 years ago, notably the rawness of the type impression, Kitching's composition has an impressionistic colour quality that would have been impossible to achieve back then. The essential lesson of Kitching's work is to use the past as a gateway to the present and to tap into it in order to achieve personal typographic expression.

⊠ Alan Kitching, 1999
Baseline magazine

Vernacular
Language of commerce

_____ In the 1980s, graphic designer Tibor Kalman defined a
genre of typography that was made up of the 'vernacular' letters
used in everyday communications. Kalman decided that graphic
design, like any other language or means of communication, had
its own informal dialects or vernacular forms. To illustrate this point,
his studio M&Co would use, for example, untutored Chinese-menu
designs and plastic message-board letters in more formal design
pieces. Another separate vernacular approach called 'retro' uses
stylized types from the first half of the twentieth century. But for
our purposes, 'vernacular' denotes a combination of stylized and
untutored practices, derived from the commercial-art printers and
type shops of the past.

Designers must use vernacular appropriately, retaining some
reference to the original time and place, or else it will look anachronistic.
This dictum is borne out by Elvio Gervasi's elaborate Fileteado-style
typography, with stylized swirls and flowering climbing plants. Fileteado
was the graphic design vernacular of the local inhabitants of Buenos Aires.
Originally, it was designed to enliven the carts that transported fruit, milk
and bread at the end of the nineteenth century. Today, while these carts are
nostalgic, they are still emblematic of the city and its culture. It is this kind
of contemporary relevancy that forms the essence of the most compelling
vernacular typography.

Most vernacular typography was created to establish an evocative
mood or setting, or to define an identity. Building a new typographic method
on a tradition – whether high or low – and being faithful to the details of the
original ensures success.

⊠ Elvio Gervasi, 2008
'Buenos Aires Tango'

Avant-garde
Unacceptable. Feasible. Acceptable.

Typographic standards were put in place the moment moveable type was invented and they revolutionized written communications. Designers and artists have been altering old rules ever since. The problem with the term 'avant-garde', however, is that once something is described as such, it is probably no longer on the edge. The evolutionary process goes in this order: unacceptable, feasible, acceptable.

That noise could be made by increasing and decreasing the sizes and weights in one typeset word was one such unacceptable concept. Advanced by the Italian Futurists, led by F.T. Marinetti, the free arrangement of words and letters on a page, or *parole in libertà* (see page 32), was a decidedly avant-garde method of writing that would freely 'deform and refresh words', by 'cutting them short, stretching them out, reinforcing the centre or the extremities, augmenting and diminishing the number of vowels or consonants', thereby creating a graphic-phonetic experience.

The 1916 *Piedigrotta*, a poem by Futurist writer Francesco Cangiullo, inspired by a traditional Neapolitan festival that would culminate with fireworks, uses typography to illustrate the explosive thrust of Mount Vesuvius, the famous volcano that stands over the gulf of Naples. The typography noisily drowns out the old while respecting the modern machine age. It is a jab against the propriety of the day, yet ultimately this typography was adopted by advertising and commercial design. And today nobody raises an eyebrow when they see type that changes size and shape on the same page. It is a ghost of the avant-garde and one of many once progressive typography tools.

Be inspired by history

⊠ Francesco Cangiullo,
1916
Piedigrotta

The typography idea book

⊠ Priest+Grace, 2014
Newsweek magazine

Pastiche
The past as plaything

Sometimes a design problem screams out for nostalgic typography, so why not indulge the urge by playing, copying, parodying or downright stealing from the distant past? If the original was produced decades or centuries before – and is established as an iconic style – then, arguably, it demands homage. In typographic practice, artefacts are often primary sources of inspiration.

The solution design agency Priest+Grace (founded by design duo Robert Priest and Grace Lee) found for a *Newsweek* cover about Russia's contemporary, anti-Western paranoiac propaganda campaign was so obvious that any other treatment would have felt like a missed opportunity. The design team used the Kremlin 11 Pro font as the basis for the typography, accompanying President Putin, in an authoritarian pose, wielding a somewhat contorted 'iron hand'. The Constructivist posters of Alexander Rodchenko and others have been inspiring designers since the 1920s with their iconography, limited palette and aggressive structure, and Priest+Grace used that as its starting-point. 'Adding the word "propaganda" was,' Robert Priest has said, 'like a red flag to a bull.'

The designers distressed the logo panel somewhat to refer back to Soviet times and the perfect pastiche fell into place. When harkening back to the past, the design template is more or less already established and ready for playing with. The greatness of the new design then comes in balancing on the line between uninspired mimicry and intelligent interpretation.

Rococo
Artful irony

_____ **There are so many variations on the retro theme because the past offers so many options for quotation. Rococo typography is a particular treat because, whether it is or it isn't your typographic preference, it is so satisfying to look at – particularly when it is done well, with care, elegance, precision and a PUNCH.**

Russian typographer Fiodor Sumkin admitted he had a good time delving back into the archives of late nineteenth- and early twentieth-century Russia – a treasure trove of letters that exude Tsarist flamboyance. In order to achieve his goal of having a go at, of all people, former British Prime Minister, the 'iron lady' Margaret Thatcher, his philosophy was the more ornament the better. His design was for her profile in *CEO* (a Russian magazine about finance and business, much like *Fortune* in the United States) and presented some of Thatcher's more fiery quotations in a co-mingling of Byzantine, Baroque and Rococo styles. Her stern, yet mellifluous, voice is so vividly evoked by the hard-edged flourish of the ornamented type, one can almost hear her speaking the words.

You may be surprised by how many times Rococo type is a fine solution to a problem. Although it is the complete opposite of the warmly embraced modern simplicity, in small doses it retains an expressive beauty and ironic bite.

ЕСЛИ **Мои** КРИТИКИ УВИДЯТ МЕНЯ ШЕСТВУЮЩЕЙ ПО ВОДАМ ТЕМЗЫ, ОНИ СКАЖУТ. это потому что она *не умеет* плавать.

НЕ МОЖЕТ БЫТЬ никакой СВОБОДЫ, ПОКА НЕТ свободы экономики.

Мы с вами едем по дороге, а ЭКОНОМИСТЫ ПЕРЕДВИГАЮТСЯ по инфраструктуре.

ЛЮДИ думают, что НА вершине ТЕСНО что это *ЭВЕРЕСТ*

Я НЕ ЗНАЮ НИКОГО кто бы поднялся Я НА вершину без упорного труда. ЭТО И ЕСТЬ СЕКРЕТ УСПЕХА.

НА САМОМ ДЕЛЕ здесь ПОЛНО МЕСТА.

Если нужно что-то *объявить*, ПОПРОСИТЕ МУЖЧИНУ. Если нужно, что-то *сделать*, ПОПРОСИТЕ ЖЕНЩИНУ.

Be inspired by history

⊠ Fiodor Sumkin, 2010
CEO magazine

Swash
Richness of the elegant hand

Spencerian cursive was a popular style from around 1840 to the early 1920s. Designed by Platt Rogers Spencer, it was the standard handwriting script used for business and social correspondence before the advent of the typewriter. It developed from an even earlier approach to handwriting itself, when swashes were in vogue, and it implies both elegance and opulence. In the United States it also became synonymous with John Hancock's famous signature on the American Declaration of Independence and was the sign of an educated, even democratic, hand. In the nineteenth century, Spencerian penmanship manuals were common in many schools. Eventually, as script typefaces were forged in metal, the engraved Spencerian aesthetic became a staple on stationery: wedding invitations, calling cards, letterheads and bank drafts, among other things.

In the twenty-first century, swash type evokes an antique, snobby aesthetic, so it should be used sparingly. But, as the Argentinian Alejandro Paul's Burgues Script – 'an ode to the late nineteenth-century American calligrapher Louis Madarasz' – demonstrates, it also evokes an anti-digital era ironically: *burgués* is Spanish for 'bourgeois'.

For this, or any swash face, to work well, the joining of letters in a fluid and flexible way is essential. It's one thing for the typeface designer to make effective typography, and quite another to avoid overdoing the design. Paul wrote: 'I can only imagine what steady nerves and discipline Madarasz must have had to be able to produce fully flourished and sublimely connected words and sentences.' These are important cautionary words for anyone trying it on their own: to make sublime typography you must combine skill with patience.

⊠ Alejandro Paul, 2011
Burgues Script

Digital
Not about bitmapping

The digital revolution in type and printing is the most powerful tsunami to have hit typographic shores since Johannes Gutenberg's invention gave rise to widespread literacy. And just as incunabula, the earliest form of printing, looks exquisitely primitive by today's standards, a similarly embryonic stage occurred in digital design. *Emigre* magazine is, arguably, 'digi-cunabula', and digital-type foundry Emigre Fonts' earliest bitmap typefaces, Oakland, Universal, Emperor, Emigre (originally from 1985, but retooled, extended and repackaged as Lo-Res in 2001), are akin to Gutenberg's first moveable types.

Typefaces designed by Czech-born type-designer Zuzana Licko during the early days of the computer bear the hallmarks of limited technology. It was noted in an Emigre Fonts specimen booklet that the look of Licko's landmark typefaces would prove 'incomprehensible to those who were not around in 1985'. The tool used to produce it, the Macintosh computer, had just appeared on the scene and its restrictions were many. The base memory was 512k, it lacked a hard drive, most data was transferred from one computer to another using floppy disks, and the screen was tiny.

Matrix, designed in 1986, was a spiky-edged postscript face made for coarse-resolution laser printers. PostScript, released in 1985, was a programming language developed by Adobe, which replaced bitmap-based fonts and made possible the drawing of glyphs as Bézier-curve outlines, which could then be rendered at any size or resolution. The release of Altsys's Fontographer, a PostScript-based font-editing software, allowed more precise drawing of letterforms.

Today, there is no functional reason for using bitmapped typefaces other than nostalgia, as they appear quaint, if not sadly out of date. Yet the faces are still available and, when applied in the right context, can add – three decades after they became **passé** – a curiously refreshing quality to a layout.

Emperor 8

Oakland 8

Emigre 10

Universal 19

☒ Zuzana Licko, 1985/2001
Lo-Res

Explore media and technique

Jonny Hannah / Jon Gray / A.M. Cassandre / Seymour Chwast / Paul Cox / Nicklaus Troxler /
Sascha Hass / Ben Barry

Hand-lettering
The first digital types

There have always been hand-drawn letters of some kind. Yet, as stylistic currency in typography, hand-lettering has gone in and out of fashion. Over the past two decades, however, hand-lettering has not only held its ground, it has increased in popularity among designers and students. The current approach is not precisionist custom lettering but rather illustrative, interpretive and expressive characters created more often by illustrators than by type-designers or typographers. Frequently, the results are interpretive copies of antique or vintage commercial typefaces.

English illustrator Jonny Hannah's lettering sums up this trend. His preference for shadow typefaces, in particular, allows for illustrative variety. You might say that Hannah's approach is the original 'digital' lettering, since it is accomplished with ten digits on two hands rather than through computer code. His work recalls various historical genres, including poster art, in which word and picture are integrated into a single entity.

The joy of hand-lettering is that virtually any method, from illustrative to calligraphic, is possible, and any combination thereof. The important thing is to choose the references from which the lettering derives carefully and make certain that it is appropriate to the assignment at hand. Hand-lettering existing typefaces amounts to a representation of the real thing – it is not real type. So, never copy a typeface for total accuracy; always leave space for imagination to reign.

☒ Jonny Hannah, 2011
'Lord Have Mercy'

LORD HAVE MERCY AH'M BURNING A HOLE WHERE I LAY!

ELVIS PRESLEY

Explore media and technique

EVERYTHING IS ILLUMINATED

'A ZESTFULLY IMAGINED NOVEL OF WONDERS... HE WILL WIN YOUR ADMIRATION, AND HE WILL BREAK YOUR HEART'
JOYCE CAROL OATES

JONATHAN SAFRAN FOER

ISBN 0-241-14166-4

9 780241 141663

The typography Idea book

Brush scrawl
Expression without (many) rules

The precision of computer typography has given rise to a rebellious trend towards imprecision and imperfection. Scrawled letterforms that were unacceptable – even in sketches, still less in formal graphic design – just a few decades ago, are now embraced as part of a DIY aesthetic. Of course, even hand-drawn scrawls end up being rendered on the computer, but the scrawl can be an effective component in a typographic scheme in which the words must have impact. By the sheer act of making them, scrawls are imbued with expressive qualities, yet the extent to which this is manifest depends a lot on how the brush is used – and whether it is hard, medium or soft.

UK designer Jon Gray (aka Gray318) holds his brush in the manner of a graffiti artist who has just defaced a picture of an unpopular autocrat. His scrawled title for the bestselling book *Everything is Illuminated* is, nevertheless, quite mannered insofar as the letters deliberately alternate between thick and thinner, with upper and lower case together in the same word.

This approach is good. When making scrawled titles, there needs to be evidence of the typographer's hand rather than generic writing. And for the most authentic result, handwriting all the words in a lighter line or slightly different style is advantageous, too.

⊠ Jon Gray, 2002
Everything is Illuminated

Custom
Licence to break rules

The same rules regarding legibility and readability are applicable when creating hand-lettering as when producing real type. With type design, rigorous standards facilitate perfection. With hand-lettering, however, the designer or illustrator has greater licence to be loose, because a particular style of letter or word will probably be used just once (and usually only for display).

The master of French poster art and designer of the iconic typefaces Peignot and Bifur, A.M. Cassandre, often drew his own letters on posters in a style that defined French art deco. He frequently overlapped sans-serif letters to create dimensional illusions. Illusions of this kind give typography its allure. He also mixed different shapes and colours to achieve eye-catching effects. This typographic approach was (and is) well suited to advertising display, as demonstrated by this poster for Pivolo aperitif, which exudes a carnival-like playfulness.

The distinctive complexity of this advertisement telegraphs a brand while connecting with the viewer through surprise. And yet, for all the licence-taking of the letter compositions, Cassandre employs geometric precision. The letters are designed on a grid and, although they have an ad hoc quality, every component of the letters lines up with the bird, which is poised to consume the aperitif. The Os echo the bird's eye and the V the bird's beak in the glass. Cassandre could not have achieved such effective design using standard type. When creating customized letters, the focus must be on the relationship of each letter to the overall composition.

⊠ A.M. Cassandre, 1924
Pivolo

Logo type
Distinguished identity

Since all of us in the West use the same Latin alphabet, the challenge for a typographic-logo designer developing a letter- or word-mark is to distinguish one mark from all the others.

There is only one IBM logo, for example, but the typeface that Paul Rand selected was Georg Trump's City Bold (and Outline), which had scores of other applications. What set it indelibly apart from the others in the same type family was Rand's introduction of parallel (or scan) lines. This had various advantages as an identity icon, including serving as a mnemonic. This logo has provided instant recognition for the IBM brand, almost unchanged, for over half a century.

Likewise, the 1964 'a' logo for the Artone ink label and box, by Seymour Chwast, has just a single letter to represent the product's distinct personality. The logo appears to be a perfect fit for the product, but the idea did not just fall into Chwast's talented hands: it was inspired by the swirls of Art Nouveau and custom-drawn by Chwast, who transformed the 'a' from a mere letter into a logo; by integrating symbol, the letter goes from anonymous to unmistakable. The concept is at once surprising and familiar, which is the hallmark of an effective logo. The 'a' suggests the ink itself; the curvaceous black form vividly represents what can be accomplished using India ink. To underscore the concept, the counter (or negative) space in the lower-case 'a' resembles a drop of ink. Imbued in this single 'a' is a wealth of information that, for Artone, was worth its weight in gold.

Not every letter or product will lend itself to as seamless a marriage of symbolism and form in its logo, but the typographic-logo designer's job is to explore and create the characteristics that might lead to a successful coupling.

⊠ Seymour Chwast, 1964
Artone Studio India Ink

Crayon
Expression with wax and grease

Marketed at children, basic crayons are not usually considered a medium for letter-making or typography. But the crayon is, historically, one of the most fundamental tools in the graphic-arts toolkit. It was with a litho-crayon, or grease pencil, that the masters of *fin de siècle* French lithographic poster design made their masterpieces. And traditionally, in a slightly less lofty manner, red or blue crayons were a designer's primary markers for writing production instructions.

The common litho-crayon may no longer be used as much in the digital age, but, like chalk, coloured crayons are part of today's lettering world. Whatever the brand or type of crayon, it allows for a fluid, handwritten line with as much or as little self-expression as desired. Sometimes, this informal lettering is appropriate to offset a more formal image or message; other times it signals that the message is not official, academic or corporate.

When the French painter and designer Paul Cox created posters with handwritten text for the Opéra National de Lorraine's 2000–01 season, informality made sense given the art, music and cultural genre that he was promoting. There was, however, another agenda: he wanted to echo the style of some paintings he was concurrently making in his studio. The handwritten crayon lettering fitted well with a series he was doing of simple stencilled shapes, inspired by Hans Arp and Ellsworth Kelly. Cox's choice of handwritten script, which he had previously used only in text, was, he explained, foremost a formal concern: 'I wished to create a fragile linear contrast to the solid blocks of colour. I also wished to experiment in poster size with handwriting.'

Crayons might be for play, but they are not just for children. The medium may not *be* the message, but crayons can help push the message to some interesting places.

☒ Paul Cox, 2000
Opéra National
de Lorraine, Nancy

à l'Opéra
l'Isola disabitata

Joseph Haydn

Opéra de Nancy et de Lorraine
19, 25, 28 avril, 2 mai 2001 à 20h00
et 22 avril 2001 à 16h00
Renseignements : 03 83 85 33 11

Nancy, 🏛 █   Mezzo MGEL

Orchestre

Saison 2000-2001

Orchestre Symphonique et Lyrique de Nancy
03 83 85 30 60

Nancy, 🏛 █

à l'Opéra
Peter Grimes

Benjamin Britten

Opéra de Nancy et de Lorraine
12, 14, 17, 19 octobre 2000 à 20h00
et 22 octobre 2000 à 16h00
renseignements : 03 83 85 33 11

Nancy, 🏛 █   MGEL

à l'Opéra
Saison 2000-2001

Peter Grimes Falstaff Cecilia
Les Pensionnaires Manon
l'Isola disabitata Fidelio

Opéra de Nancy et de Lorraine
03 83 85 30 60

Nancy, 🏛 █   MGEL

Blackboard
Chalk that talks

The smell of chalk dust used to be a constant in primary-school classrooms and college lecture halls. It was also a tool of the 'chalk talker', speakers who performed using chalk drawings and writings as visual aids. Today, the whiteboard has replaced the blackboard, and erasable markers are the teacher's writing implements of choice. However, blackboard chalk, which was introduced during the very early nineteenth century, has returned with a vengeance in the twenty-first. No longer a classroom staple, chalk is frequently used for a slew of illustrative lettering and stylized scribbles. Chalking it up might, nonetheless, fall into the category of graphic-design conceits that light up the skies for an instant and gradually disappear. Unless, that is, new methods result in new styles.

Much blackboard lettering *du jour* follows the currently fashionable formula of quaintly and colourfully recreating vintage wood types and decorative cartouches. The aesthetic is appealing in a nostalgic way and can be mistaken for pastiche (see page 46). So, when using chalk as a typographic tool, do not simply follow trends – discover a personal 'chalk' voice.

One such voice is Niklaus Troxler's, whose 2011 poster for the Lucien Dubuis Trio has a frenetic improvisational tone appropriate for promoting jazz musicians. Blackboard chalk gives typographers licence to be 'precisely imprecise'. The lettering in this poster is obviously ad libbed, devoid of stylistic effect, yet full of visual energy and totally in sync with the pictures and marks that represent the trio's unique blend of sax, bass and drum sounds.

Troxler's poster looks like a rough sketch. But, given the expressive freedom that chalk writing encourages, it doesn't matter, as long as it communicates its message.

⊠ Nicklaus Troxler, 2011
Lucien Dubuis Trio

Vector
One bézier at a time

'Vectorizing' existing letterforms is surprisingly simple, thanks to Adobe Illustrator. A good-quality scan is all that's needed to launch a process that takes only a few basic steps. The resulting vector type – type made of individual points connected by lines and curves – is manipulated as individual letters rather than as a keyable font, allowing designers to be more 'hands-on'. Each letterform is easily sized and positioned individually, compelling designers to slow down and consider decisions more deliberately. It's a different experience to traditional typesetting and is, in some ways, more fun.

Creating vector type from scratch, one Bézier curve at a time, is even more satisfying – and challenging, requiring a higher level of expertise. Its reward is maximum originality, creativity and flexibility, but conjuring vector type from scratch requires dedication and practice, as well as an intimate knowledge of the basic tenets of typography.

Designer Sascha Hass created his award-winning ampersand poster in Illustrator, connecting a dense array of points to form a fine and intricate spider's web. His intention was to represent, by joining together points on a computer screen, how connections that are forged in the world generate their strength organically.

Typical typeface design seeks to create idealized and elegant forms, and does so by using as few points as possible. Hass has gone 'gangbusters' in the opposite direction, creating a fine tapestry of intersecting lines, while at the same time preserving the graceful shape of the original ampersand. Simplicity meets complexity, as if we are viewing a wire frame for a 3-D character design.

⊠ Sascha Hass, 2013
Das Spinnennetz
('The Spider's Web')

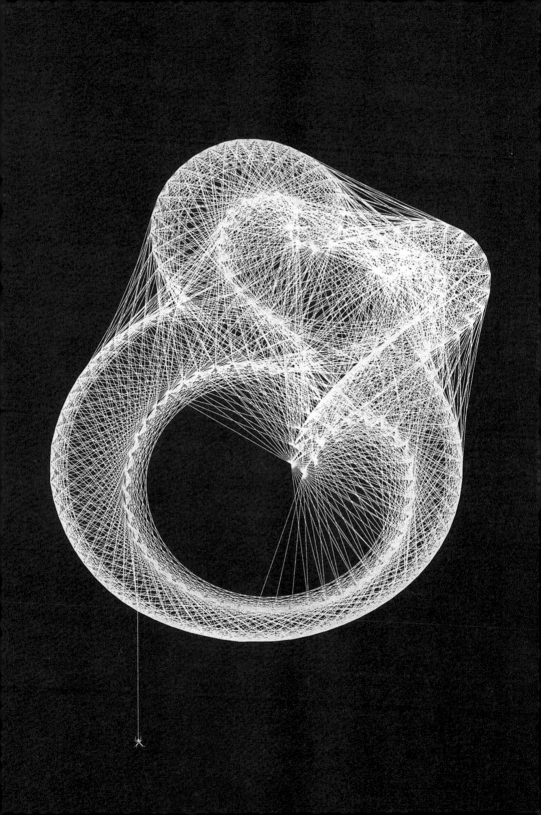

⊠ Ben Barry, 2015
'Howdy'

Laser
The joy of precision

In the 1950s, the word on the street was that the future would be governed by laser technology. Today, the future has arrived and typography includes laser optics that can create letterforms and patterns with focused beams of light directed at paper, fabric and wood. The process does recall the science fiction of the 1950s: beams burn or vaporize substances using a gas jet, leaving sharp, clean edges that would be difficult to replicate by hand. It is no longer fiction. The facility to make intricate designs with pinpoint accuracy has opened up opportunities for typographers on everything from wedding invitations to wine labels. Laser-cutting has been used to fashion typographic scarves and pendants, turning letterforms into wearable objects, and to make usable furniture.

The origin of this method is paper-cutting, which dates back to sixth-century China. Later, having become popular with society women in eighteenth-century American colonies, it spread to other classes, becoming a staple of folk art. Laser-cutting is simply paper-cutting on steroids. And Ben Barry's 'Howdy' poster amply exemplifies this 'steroid-driven' evolutionary shift. It was created for a lecture at the Dallas Society of Visual Communications in Texas so that Artifacture, a laser-cutting vendor, could showcase its capabilities. Barry created a poster, pushed the technology to its limits and opened up new options for all typographers with access to the right machines.

Laser-cutting is the intersection between print design and state-of-the-art technology. It allows the creation of tactile and dimensional typography, expanding the possibilities for how letterforms can be used outside traditional print applications. Typographers take note: you can now, finally, retire your X-Acto knives.

Create illusion and mystique

Michiel Schuurman / Paul Sych / Zsuzsanna Ilijin / Stephen Doyle

Flat dimensional
The mystique of illusion

If a piece of typography or text is memorable, then logic suggests it must have been readable. However, illusion can also contribute to its being memorable. Sigmund Freud maintained that illusion derives its strength 'from the fact that it falls in with our instinctual desires', and designers have an instinctive desire to create dimensions on flat surfaces. Granted, this may not be one of life's most fundamental desires, but typographers and designers are hardwired to meet every challenge – and creating illusion is one of them.

Transforming a two-dimensional (flat) surface into a three-dimensional opportunity is engaging for both designer and viewer, and also attainable. When done with elegance and an element of surprise, it can also be laudable: 'The Catalyst's Agenda', Michiel Schuurman's poster for the Hotel Maria Kapel in the Netherlands, achieves dimensionality through intense rendering and tapping into what look as if they are the natural folds of the paper. Schuurman says it is the result of experimentation. Indeed, there are no tried-and-tested recipes for creating dimensional magic.

The impact, however, is worth the effort. Remember, unexpected and successful illusion invariably leaves a mental cookie that locks a typographic message securely in the memory bank of the beholder.

⊠ Michiel Schuurman, 2010
'The Catalyst's Agenda'

THE CATALYSTS AGENDA

Create illusion and mystique

the Deep

(141)

Time stands still in the presence
of arcane beauty. Submerged beneath
reflections of water and light, movement and mysticism are
captured in brilliant colour
Photography by
MIKE RUIZ

Fluidity
Liquid and digital

The concept of 'fluidity' might immediately suggest letterforms that are made using real liquid, or, perhaps, those that are digitally rendered to evoke fluid. Type can be made to drip, splatter, ooze, melt or run. In practice, liquefying type is usually achieved through the magic of Photoshop, but there are occasions on which ink and water are manipulated using a pin or fine brush to create forms that bleed. In other words, the options available to you will flow if you turn on the creative tap.

In Paul Sych's 'the Deep' feature opener for *fshnunlimited* (*f.u.*) magazine, the designer submerges the headline under water, creating a typographical ripple effect. Sych's intention was not to overpower the Mike Ruiz photograph on the facing page, but rather to create a dialogue between word and image that results in a single visual voice, with the shape and geometry of the letterforms meant to mimic the rhythmic pulses of waves.

There are many variations on this theme that have been explored in both editorial and advertising media. Maybe because water is one of the most basic elements it appeals to us on a primal level. Or perhaps it just looks cool and refreshing. Fluid type evokes a natural force and adds a heightened sense of movement to any page or screen.

⊠ Paul Sych, 2014
fshnunlimited magazine

Create illusion and mystique

Overprinting
Ghosting and highlighting

If you are staring at the image on the opposite page and finding it hard to fathom, don't worry, there is nothing wrong with your eyes, nor are you seeing double (or triple), and there are no dark objects obstructing your vision. This is an example of overprinting, a process in which colours, shapes, patterns and other marks are laid on and around type. It is a very common way to implant graphic richness and dimension in a composition that might otherwise be too ordinary, or one that simply demands layers of 'stuff'.

Overprinting is a process of harvesting the sort of make-ready printing errors that have now become deliberate graphic-design tropes. One attribute that lends overprinting a certain cachet is ghosting type, which injects a mysterious air to words. Conversely, there is also the sort of overprinting that actually helps to highlight words and phrases. It's a good tool to use when establishing sensations of dynamic transparency. And, while overprinting is a routine feature of graphic design, it can be used effectively and pleasingly to complement typography as well.

This A0-size silkscreen-poster print, 'Where are the Flying Cars?', designed by Zsuzsanna Ilijin and produced by hand at graphic-design studio AGA in Amsterdam, included the efforts of six designers who were asked to make a poster with four colour layers. The concept behind it is that by the year 2010, when the poster was originally produced, science fiction had predicted the advent of flying cars. There are still no flying cars, but the layers help frame the bold and comic, variously sized lettering.

The typography idea book

78

⊠ Zsuzsanna Ilijin, 2010
'Where are the Flying Cars?'

Shadow
Turning on the light and the dark

The 1940s marked the golden age of noir film, a genre of mystery, murder and suspense that contrasted extremes of light and shadow on screen for dramatic impact. Usually, film titles for noir films expressed their characteristically dark aesthetic through slab serif, shadow and script typography that was often lit with a light source that heightened the melodrama. Today, these title cards and sequences occupy a special place in the typographic pantheon because they continue to be revived and esteemed by successive generations.

For designers who are fans of films and their titles, the noir style is deeply ingrained in their consciousness. In addition to its emotional resonance, the strength of shadow type is that it is at once retro *and* contemporary, which must account for its most recent revival.

New York designer Stephen Doyle is not a slave to retro fashions but he appreciates the power of three dimensions, and photographic manipulation of handmade shadow type is a staple of his repertoire. The 'Enemy' typography is handcrafted in wood (not rendered in Photoshop) then melodramatically lit and photographed, to create noir's signature eerie, studied effect. The black and white goes against current preference for colourful designs but the sacrifice is well worth it. 'Enemy' comes to the fore in a satisfyingly threatening way, not just emphasizing but rejoicing in the charged word.

The noir approach provides today's designer and typographer with a means of creating a sense of anticipation in the audience, just like the noir film titles did as they announced the melodrama to follow.

⊠ Stephen Doyle, 2004
'Enemy'

Create illusion and mystique

Experiment with style and form

El Lissitzky / Wim Crouwel / Experimental Jetset / Wing Lau / Josef Müller-Brockmann /
Herbert Bayer / Áron Jancsó

Experimental
Changing the look of language

There are many ways to read text. Not everyone scans from left to right. Not all alphabets have twenty-six letters. Challenging norms is essential to maintaining any living language, and the language of typography is no exception. Some of the twentieth century's most audacious experimentation was attempted during the late 1910s and early 1920s, during a period of revolutionary fever in Russia and Europe. The 1917 Russian Revolution triggered a series of typographic tremors throughout Europe that were particularly potent in the hearts and minds of the Russian Constructivists, among whom El Lissitzky was a leading *provocateur*.

His cover for *Object* (the Berlin-based tri-lingual design and culture journal aimed at a European readership) championed Constructivist and Suprematist art and remains the *pièce de résistance* of revolutionary typographic language. It is a model for how pushing the standards of typography can change the look of language itself. To experiment means to attempt feats never tackled before. It also means you have a licence to fail. Lissitzky's *Object* is now classic, though it was a risk at the time to employ abstract geometry in combination with recognizable typefaces.

When experimenting typographically, it is useful to retain some familiar hook so the reader is not entirely at sea, and then play with shapes and materials in such a way that the surprising elements can be understood. Never leave the end-user out in the cold. You should understand the needs and tolerances of the audience, as Lissitzky did, so that, even though the result may initially shock the system, the user or viewer will come to appreciate the challenge.

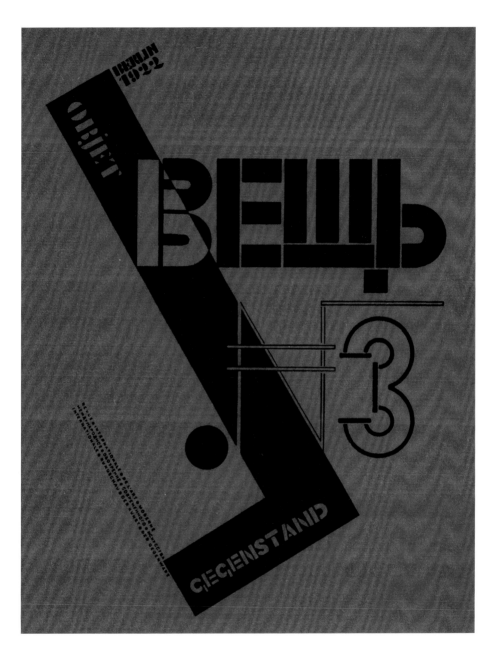

⊠ El Lissitzky, 1922
Object

neu
alphabet

a	een	une	eine
possibility	mogelijkheid	possibilite	moglichkeit
for	voor	pour	fur
the	de	le	die
new	nieuwe	developpement	neue
development	ontwikkeling	nouveau	entwicklung

an
introduction
for
a
programmed
typography

Smart type
More than beautiful

Smart type is exactly what you think it is. It's type that makes you wish you'd created it yourself – type that has its origins in such a great (and often simple) idea that you smack yourself on the head for not thinking of it first. Smart type is more than beautiful: it's type that is intellectually deliberate.

Dutch designer Wim Crouwel is particularly well known for his use of grid-based layouts and clean, legible typography but he has also enjoyed exploring areas outside typographic traditions. His 1967 New Alphabet was a personal project intended to create an experimental alphabet of horizontal and vertical strokes, using the cathode-ray tube technology that was employed by early monitors and phototypesetting equipment. The typeface sparked a debate about typography as art, and was received with mixed reactions by the design community. Crouwel responded by saying that his New Alphabet was never really meant to be used, but was instead a statement about traditional typography and the new digital technology.

Crouwel's New Alphabet is smart because it was driven by the technology it was commenting on, and both the possibilities and limitations of technology are considered simultaneously. Smart type is purposeful in its activity, creating its own set of rules and, as technologies make it easier for designers to make typefaces, opportunities for re-examination and adaptation can only increase for the twenty-first-century typographer.

Experiment with style and form

⊠ Wim Crouwel, 1967
    New Alphabet

Lower case
The sculpture of negative space

A bicameral alphabet, including our own Latin-based system, is composed of large (majuscule) and small (minuscule) letters that, during hot-metal times, were compartmentalized by size and family in separate upper and lower drawers, or type cases. From this was derived the standard nomenclature, upper case and lower case. These variations have been so essential to the Western writing system that it is hard to conceive of one case without the other. But, for over a century, linguistic reformers have argued that the bicameral system should be simplified, if not transformed entirely. In 1928, the progressive German Bauhaus proclaimed on its letterhead that they wrote everything in lower case to save time: 'Why use capital letters if we don't use them when we speak?'

They had a point. German writing was extraordinarily hard to learn and read, because spiky Fraktur types were burdensome in appearance and also because caps were required on all nouns. So, with the advent of the archetypical modern system known as The New Typography, not only was Fraktur unacceptable, but also only lower-case alphabets were promoted. This was because sans-serif lower case was presumed to be easier to learn and more economical to use as the act of typesetting was simplified.

During the 1940s, Swiss modernist designers began using all lower-case headlines. Lower case was perceived as being more modern than serif faces or, at least, more casual in appearance than upper-case settings from the same type family. Experimental Jetset's 'net zo blind als wij' ('Just as Blind as We Are') poster for De Theatercompagnie proves that using a large, lower-case bold grotesque headline is not merely powerful but sculptural: the characters that form the typographic unit engage comfortably in the sea of negative white space.

Critics will argue that using only one lower-case grotesque typeface, stacked flush left, is hardly very creative typography, but try to do this with the same level of precision and you'll realize that making a poster with such neutral type appear eye-catching is a true challenge.

net

de theater compagnie gilgamesj

zo
blind
als
wij

De Theatercompagnie
25 januari t/m 26 maart 2005

Regie: Theu Boermans
Tekst: Raoul Schrott
Vertaling: Tom Kleijn

Het Compagnietheater
Kloveniersburgwal 50
Amsterdam

reserveren 020 5205320
www.theatercompagnie.nl
info@theatercompagnie.nl

Spelers:
Anneke Blok
Theu Boermans
Stefaan Degand
Bracha van Doesburgh
Casper Gimbrère
Fedja van Huêt
Myranda Jongeling
Jeroen van Koningsbrugge
Hans Leendertse
Ruben Lürsen
Harry van Rijthoven
Lineke Rijxman

Experiment with style and form

⊠ Experimental Jetset,
2004
'net zo blind als wij'

MENACE by Chris Yee

Debuting as his first solo exhibition, Chris Yee invites you into his world of Misinterpreted Americana, parallel universes, rap royalty and bitter rivalries where everyone is a menace.

Including a year long collection of black and white ink work, Chris explores techniques familiar to stylings of 90's comics, punk, rap and gang aesthetics.

Opening reception:
6pm Wednesday
6 November 2013

Continues daily until:
11am–7pm Sunday
10 November 2013

Presented by:
kind of — gallery

Venue:
kind of — gallery
70 Oxford Street
Darlinghurst NSW

Sponsored by:
Magners Australia

☒ Wing Lau, 2013
'Menace'

Minimalism
Less and more

_____ 'Less is more' was a concept introduced to the design vocabulary in the early 1960s by the architect Ludwig Mies van der Rohe and, ever since, this century-defining dictum has been the philosophical underpinning of modern design. While Mies meant that excessive ornament was _verboten_ on buildings, there is a little more leeway in typographic minimalism, which can range from devout fealty to seminal letterform proportions to more modest concepts of clarity.

Wing Lau pursues clarity through simplicity. His practice adheres to the maxim 'design is in the content' (or, put another way, 'the solution is in the problem'). In the minimalist form, shape, rhythm and composition of his poster for 'Menace', the debut solo exhibition of illustrator Chris Yee, Lau looked for typographic solutions in the artist's distinctive work, which explores techniques reminiscent of 1990s comics – black-and-white drawings crammed with the detail and hypnotic textures familiar in punk, rap and gang aesthetics. Yee's complex imagery reflects contemporary society in a time of menace. Lau's challenge was to represent Yee, yet not to use any of his detailed work.

Minimalism is not as simple as setting a line of Helvetica or Univers on an empty grid – boring layout is never the answer. Lau based his poster image on the grid structure of comic books. Each panel forms an abstracted letter comprising the word 'Menace' and reveals a reductive process that results in a black, bold and powerful, yet minimalist, image.

Expressive reduction
Most impact for least characters

Swiss typography (aka International Style) is considered cold, sterile and lacking in expression. Wrong! Although some of the emblematic sans-serif typefaces, Akzidenz-Grotesk, Univers and Helvetica, are reasonably neutral, and some corporate applications of the Swiss Style exhibit a visual sameness, the myth of monotony has been disproved in so many of the posters, brochures and publications under the International umbrella.

Swiss designer Josef Müller-Brockmann, who authored the quintessential book on the universal grid system and stands as a pioneer of the International Style, was not content with formulaic typography. 'Order was always wishful thinking for me,' he told *Eye* magazine in 1995. 'The formal organization of the surface by means of the grid, a knowledge of the rules that govern legibility (line length, word and letter spacing and so on) and the meaningful use of colour are among the tools a designer must master in order to complete his or her task in a rational and economic matter.' So where does typographic expression enter this equation?

His 1960 poster 'Weniger Lärm' ('Less Noise', a public-awareness message) seamlessly integrates Swiss typography and emotive photography in an iconic way. The type, which is laid over the image at a startling angle, appears to be emanating from the tortured woman's pained body. In this reductive composition, Müller-Brockmann captures the cause and the effect of the emotional pain and triggers empathy from the poster's audience.

It is unnecessary to add anything more. The type and image pairing does its job without extraneous visual tropes. However, a designer should be wary of following the style 'verbatim', as the outcome will be impersonal. Integrating the spirit of this style into a typographic treatment that is itself unique will expand the boundaries of the style and ensure its visual allure.

⊠ Josef Müller-Brockmann,
1960
'Weniger Lärm'

The typography idea book

Grids
Making letter boxes

Design is based on establishing boundaries. The grid is the framework that delineates the boundaries of type and image on a page. It also symbolizes the early days of hand-typesetting, when type slugs were stored in a type case – a grid by any other name.

Herbert Bayer, the Austrian–American Bauhaus teacher and a leading modernist designer, may have had this symbolism in mind when he designed the poster for the 'Europäisches Kunstgewerbe 1927' exhibition in Leipzig, Germany. Leipzig is one of the great printing centres and so the symbolism was entirely apt. Another, perhaps ancillary, reason could be that a poster with just type like this clearly stands apart from other illustrated typographic placards.

The coloured boxes form a curiously hypnotic pattern that impacts the viewer on two levels: first, in the readability of such a long title – the eye follows the letters as though each were a separate image – and then, second, the brain cognitively arranges them all together into the individual words of the title.

Grids are an essential part of the design equation. They act as an invisible armature on which typography is composed. The grid maintains order and structure. Some typographers have a free-form style, but, for strict type and graphic design, a grid must always be in the equation. And, as strict as it may be, there are scores of grid possibilities available. Remember that, while a grid is an effective frame of containment, it is not a vice. Grids are disciplinary tools, not just for the designer who has to create within their constraints, but also for the audience, which is made to play a simple, perceptual game, hopscotching from one typographical box to the next.

⊠ Herbert Bayer, 1927
'Europäisches
Kunstgewerbe 1927'

Abstraction
Legibility be damned

The common wisdom is that readers should not be distracted by the form, style or composition of typefaces. The aim should always be for clarity in as aesthetically pleasing a way as possible. Or should it?

Typographers throughout the nineteenth, twentieth and twenty-first centuries have rebelled against the presumption that typographic purity should be maintained at all costs. Unreadable, yet still legible, typesetting has been a cornerstone of this typographic revolution. Although many of its ideas have been shown to be passing trends, attempts at promoting abstract form as a new typography have been beneficial, if only to continually test the limits of typographic potential.

Most recently, many designers have weighed into computer technology with radical ideas of how type might play a larger role in expressive communications. Hungarian designer Áron Jancsó's *Qalto* flows and leaps like freestyle jazz. The letters and ligatures are composed of very thin hairlines and very thick elements. This high contrast produces a stunning visual effect and a unique optical rhythm. Jancsó says, 'Some words have good rhythm and others don't,' and he has therefore used various weights. The face, which recalls early Surrealist and abstract painting, is both eye-catching and impactful.

Typographic abstraction only succeeds when there is an anchor in the real world. The look can be anarchic but its message should not be entirely obscured by an artistic impulse. Abstraction should be used as the hook that leads you to the information.

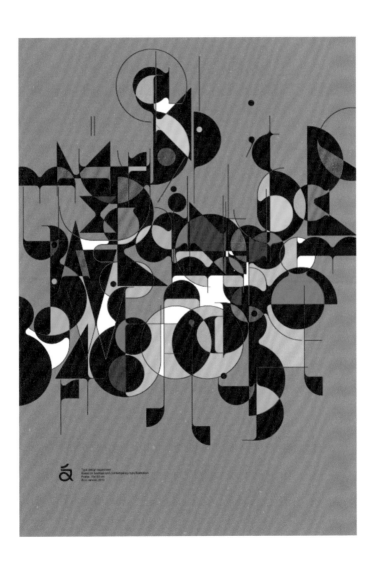

⊠ Áron Jancsó, 2012
Qalto

Play and improvise

Jamie Reid / Tom Carnase / Milton Glaser / Rizon Parein /
Roger Excoffon / Paul Belford / Alexander Vasin / Lester Beall /
Neville Brody / Eric Gill / Tom Eckersley

Ransom notes
Clipped improvisational type

The ransom note, among the most familiar typographic clichés, used to be the way kidnappers and other criminals communicated their demands while remaining anonymous. It was also a typographic tool of the Italian Futurists and European Dadaists in their printed missives and manifestoes. Which came first? Possibly, it was actually the Cubists, whose paintings sometimes included snippets of lettering from newspapers and magazines.

What came last, or at least more recently, was the punk style of lettering that deliberately broke the rules of typographic propriety. Specifically, there was English designer Jamie Reid's renowned cover design for the Sex Pistol's single 'God Save the Queen', which established ransom-note lettering as the archetype of punk styling and, eventually, as one its most recognized clichés.

There are still various ways of 'riffing' on the ransom-note approach today, even if Reid's 'classic' kidnapper version is the most familiar. Clipped-letter typography can be an effective method beyond punk if a design would entirely fail to convey its message without it. Because it is a trope that comes with its own symbolic baggage (namely its association with criminals and punks), the method should be used sparingly and wisely. Yet, just because it has inherent references, should not put you off entirely.

⊠ Jamie Reid, 1977
'God Save the Queen'

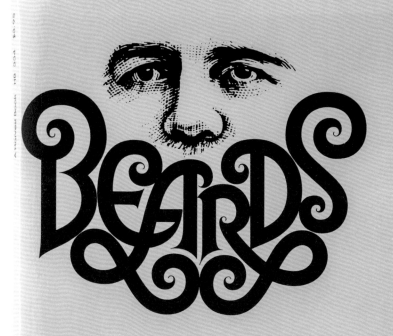

A Harvest book   HG 334 $3.95

Reginald Reynolds

The fascinating history of beards through the ages.
"First-rate entertainment." —San Francisco Chronicle

Puns
Two meanings, one seamless image

There are few more satisfying typographic experiences than when a designer stumbles upon a visual pun. The pun is at once one of the most common of all designer tools and the most difficult to accomplish without it being a cliché. The cover for the book *Beards* is a classic of punning and a paradigm of graphic wit. This concept, conceived by Herb Lubalin, art directed by Harris Lewine and designed by Alan Peckolick, is a quintessential Lubalinesque idea in which type and lettering also comically illustrate the title.

A visual pun provides two cognitive experiences at once. In this case, the custom lettering by Tom Carnase suggests, through its stylized swashes and curlicues, a mass of facial hair and, at the same time, the word 'Beards' is entirely legible. The addition of the vintage engraving of eyes and nose reinforce the meaning with consummate elegance.

When creating a typographic pun, never force the joke but allow the word and image to evolve naturally. You'll know it when you see it. After fifty years, the reputation of this *Beards* cover continues to grow in the annals of graphic design.

Play and improvise

⊠ Alan Peckolick, Tom
Carnase, Herb Lubalin,
Harris Lewine, 1976
Beards

Rebuses
Substituting picture for word

A rebus, one of the oldest graphic tropes, is a representation of a word, sometimes a puzzle, made up of pictures or symbols that suggest the meaning of that word. If the frequency with which a rebus has been imitated is any indication, the most familiar – indeed famous – of them all is 'I [heart] New York', designed in 1977 by Milton Glaser.

The representation of love as a simple heart symbol is an image taken straight from childhood – simple, yet so meaningful. This heart never stops beating. Everyone can relate to this symbol and it can be applied to virtually anything. It is, in short, universal.

Not all rebuses are as easy to decipher as 'I [heart] NY', but as the basis for a logo or other graphic identifier, the rebus is the sine qua non of typographic devices. In many instances, the visual symbol substitutes for a word or phrase, but it might also replace only a letter. In fact, there is a preponderance of such things used as logos and titles, with the second most famous being Paul Rand's IBM made from an eye, bee and 'M'.

In recent years the technique has been employed to excess, but it remains a valuable tool. So, when using the rebus solution, it is important to make sure that, while it is playful, it is not vague. If Glaser had used anything other than a heart – red lips, for instance – the word-mark would not immediately have translated as love.

⊠ Milton Glaser, 1977
'I [heart] NY'

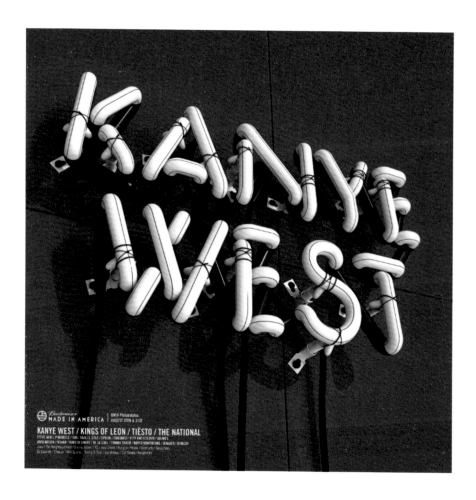

Illumination
The lighter side

Night-time is not only when the stars come out, it is also when neon signs come on. The optical sensation of being in the middle of an illuminated typographic spectacle is unforgettable and has boundless design implications. Even signs that, in daylight, seem poorly designed come alive at night with glowing neon type that floats against darkened backgrounds.

It is not as difficult as it once was to achieve this effect in print without actually photographing real neon signs. The effect of illuminating type can be achieved using Photoshop and the results are extremely convincing, whether on paper or on screen. The goal is to make the typography 'worthy' of the special effects.

Rizon Parein's sign for a Kanye West performance is a *trompe-l'oeil*, rendered using Cinema 4D and V-Ray software. The sign is not real but it looks as though it is. Parein makes type look so dimensionally believable, with such a magical glow, that it is, in fact, impossible to determine whether it exists or is only a representation.

Illuminated typography does not have to be a simulacrum. There are many other ways for two-dimensional type surfaces to emit multi-dimensional rays, but the more illusionistic the better.

⊠ Rizon Parein, 2014
'Kanye West'

Novelty
Serious fun

The term 'novelty' suggests that a typeface has unconventional or silly features, which in turn implies it is experimental or trivial. While most novelty display faces are certainly fun to use because they inject a touch of wit into layouts, some have also been serious attempts at changing the paradigms of type design. Nonetheless, novelty typefaces are not usually in currency for long stretches of time because they quickly shed their novelty. This said, there do exist a few 'classic novelties' that are often reprised for various purposes. If a design problem calls for novelty, through the selection must still be based on sophisticated criteria, and the challenge for the typographer is to avoid it being superfluous.

Whether or not Roger Excoffon's gyrating Calypso is a novelty or an experimental face (or both) can be endlessly debated, but it is a good example of a 'serious' fun face. When released by the Fonderie Olive in 1958, it had all the traits of a novelty. Its supple, curling-paper quality with bold, Benday (halftone) dot pattern, suggested a modern version of illuminated capitals. The use of visible dots to make up individual letters shows that there was a conceptual side to Calypso as well though. Creating a metal face with halftone dots that went from white to black was a technical challenge. Excoffon made sketches of the outlines of each character; shading was added by airbrush and converted to a dot-screen. Calypso's caps were cast in 20, 24, 30 and 36 point and included a full stop and a hyphen. It was, therefore, novel in more ways than one: in its manufacture and its ultimate dimensional aesthetic.

As with all novelty types, Calypso's application would be the real test. It could be either terribly engaging or depressingly dumb. Knowing when to spec such a face demands a certain level of restraint. One of Calypso's best uses was neither as a headline nor any other lengthy display, but as a two-letter logo for the early-1970s alternative culture magazine *US*: the type's hint of curling pages and halftone dots perfectly symbolized the concept of a magazine.

⊠ Roger Excoffon, 1958
Calypso

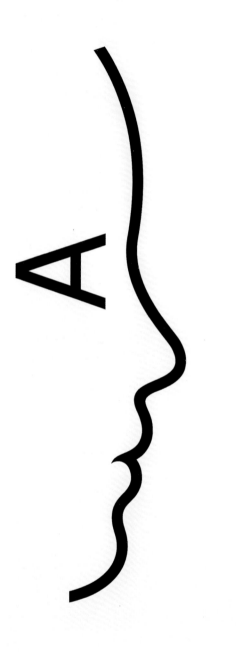

Type face
Making character portraits

Making portraits from typefaces is not even remotely essential as part of the toolkit of a truly great typographer, and yet, it is a nice extra skill to have mastered. When the typographic visage is cleverly composed it is, at the very least, satisfying to see how the juxtaposition of different letters stimulates cognitive joyfulness.

The portrait might be of a generic or an actual person, but there are many applications for this sort of typographic play. An offshoot of it is the emoticon, a shorthand means of creating a pictorial quip or graphic coda, not unlike a colophon. Basic emoticons such as happy and sad can be achieved using punctuation as facial features, for example :-) and :-(.

On a larger scale, some type face portraits involve rather complicated contortions of letters, numerals and punctuation to produce a likeness; others, such as Paul Belford's 2006 annual-awards poster for the magazine *Creative Review*, are just simple and elegant. Rather than build an entire face out of typefaces, Belford's quietly minimalist composition uses a sans-serif 'A' that immediately resembles an open eye. Part visual pun, part typographic transformation, this modest but powerful composition demands a second look – and thus ensures its memorability. Like Belford, try for a smart concept that doesn't go overboard and, when making faces, choose your characters wisely. Go for the element of surprise.

⊠ Paul Belford, 2006
Creative Review

Play and improvise

Integration
Union of art and letter

The perfect union of type and image is one of the fundamentals of good graphic design. Posters are a primary genre for exhibiting this perfection but, too often, minimalist designers place a line or two of type on the image without integrating the elements. As with a symphony, in which all the instruments play in sync, when type and image are truly in concert the result is harmonious and melodic, but can also pack a punch.

Typography succeeds and fails in the relationship between the elements, and the aim of all successful poster typography is to reach that harmonious symphonic climax. That is why Russian designer Alexander Vasin's poster from a series for Typomania 2015 , the annual conference whose aim is to build a typographic community in Moscow, is a *tour de force* of witty conceptual integration. Nothing less would be acceptable for a conference devoted to type and typography.

This example shows how the interweaving of type and image can be as freshly modern as any minimalist headline—picture combination. The success of this design is in the 'planned improvisation', in which type is made to fit naturally around and through the images (in this case a photo, but the technique could work equally well with an illustration). A graphic designer should always aim for a well-orchestrated composition that seamlessly blends message and aesthetics.

⊠ Alexander Vasin
(photograph by
Boris Bendikov), 2015
Typomania 2015

Scale
Large and small

Typographers have many choices to make, but perhaps the most critical decision concerns the scale of letters in relation to each other. The juxtaposition of large and small is crucial for creating impact. Depending on the requirements of the job, some typographic elements will logically be larger than others, as in, for example, newspaper or magazine headlines. In other situations, the typographer's instinct, aesthetic and intelligence must lead the design, with the outcome being a thoughtfully considered composition, even if the layout looks chaotic or ad hoc.

Lester Beall's 1937 cover for *PM* magazine reveals the visual impact of radical scale-shifts when they are made with the perfect typeface combinations. This timeless-looking design comprises an ornate, antique capital 'P' and a modern, lower-case slab-serif 'm'. Various symbolic meanings can be ascribed to this choice, of which the most powerful, perhaps, is that the 'P' represents the old school while the 'm' suggest machine-age modernity. The two co-exist, but the 'm' is on the rise.

It is the composition, influenced by Russian Constructivism and The New Typography, that makes the cover so dynamic. Scale, however, is not the sole component: the slightly skewed black 'm' is a startling object, while the diminutive red 'P' appears to be overshadowed, though it is, nonetheless, integral. The choice of 'P' and the two red bars may seem random, but it is the desired effect to show the juxtaposition of modern dominance over the antique. Scale is the typographer's best tool. And this example shows how an abstract typographic idea can result in strong, disciplined graphic design.

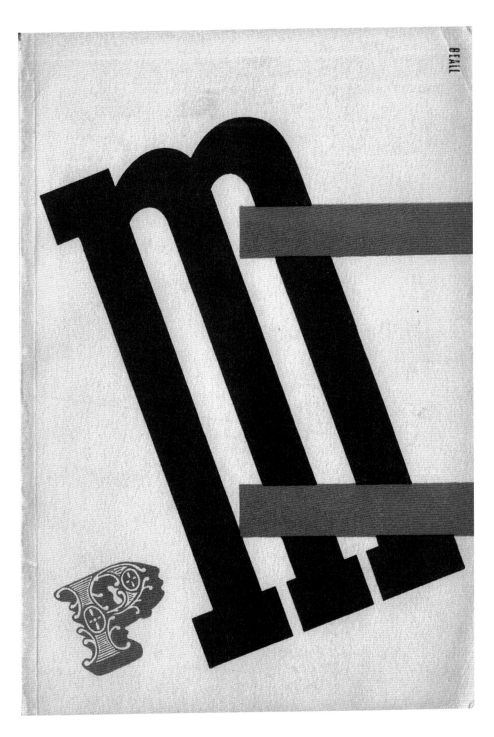

⊠ Lester Beall, 1937
PM magazine

Jumbled
Radical changes

It seems logical that radical variations in the scale of letters set within the same design, rather than set uniformly, will result in compelling juxtapositions. When it comes to typography, setting words or headlines with jumbled-sized letters together in the same layout may distract, but it can, conversely, also increase the likelihood of a text being read. It really depends on the content and context.

When UK designer Neville Brody art directed and designed the signature postmodern magazine *The Face* from 1981 to 1986, his typography was the embodiment of modernist simplicity. The controlled anarchy that pervaded his layouts released, in a sense, untamed typographic beasts, akin to when, in the 1950s, early rock 'n' roll music released the inner 'wild things' of scores of teenagers.

The music analogy is apt. Scale shifts in display type resulted from Brody's desire to capture type's rhythm and colour, and to invite the user to respond 'emotionally to the visual aspect of a text as much as to the language it embodies'. Brody told *Eye* magazine that, in creating typographic discordance, 'We're trying to extract the visual character from the written word. Scale change also impacts the basic rhythm and visual quality of type, resulting in a form of visual poetry.'

While *The Face* is emblematic of a moment in the late '80s when postmodernists rebelled against mid-century modernist purity, the lessons learned from Brody's typographic high jinks and experiments with irregular shifts in size are still applicable. Typographers have options: when typography needs to ease the user into a comfortable reading environment, scale change like this may not be ideal, but when telegraphing a sense of excitement and urgency, a designer should never 'scale' back on making typographic 'jambalaya'.

⊠ Neville Brody, 1988
Nike, Just Do It

Play and improvise

117

Initials
Letter as overture

There are few texts in which an initial cap ('drop cap') is more appropriate than in the biblical 'In the beginning . . .' Undoubtedly, the Holy Bible, and other religious manuscripts decorated by scribes, established the use of illuminated letters as a sort of typographic overture with which to lead off certain paragraphs. This practice was upheld even after the advent of the printing press, in Johannes Gutenberg's famous bibles.

Biblical initial caps were not simply ornamental frivolities. Printers, and the scribes before them, used these letters to mark where a new phrase, psalm or section began in the body of a text. While many of these earliest caps were indeed extremely ornate and illustrative, Edward Johnston's initial 'I' for the 1903 Doves Press Bible has a sublimely spare modernity that reflects fifteenth-century Venetian printing. Johnston greatly influenced Eric Gill who was known for more 'theatrical' illuminated letters such as those he used for the opening of Genesis 1:1 in *The Four Gospels*, 1931.

Any oversized letter that starts a sentence or paragraph is an initial, or drop, cap. In addition, designers have at their disposal adjacent caps, which drop to the side of a column, and raised caps, which rise above the text block. Initial caps go in and out of style rather quickly: they serve so many purposes that it is easy for typographers to use them excessively or inappropriately in a layout. When well considered, however, initials can bring contrast to a printed page, add a touch of class to a staid layout, and draw the eye where the typographer wants the reader to go.

⊠ Eric Gill, 1931
The Four Gospels

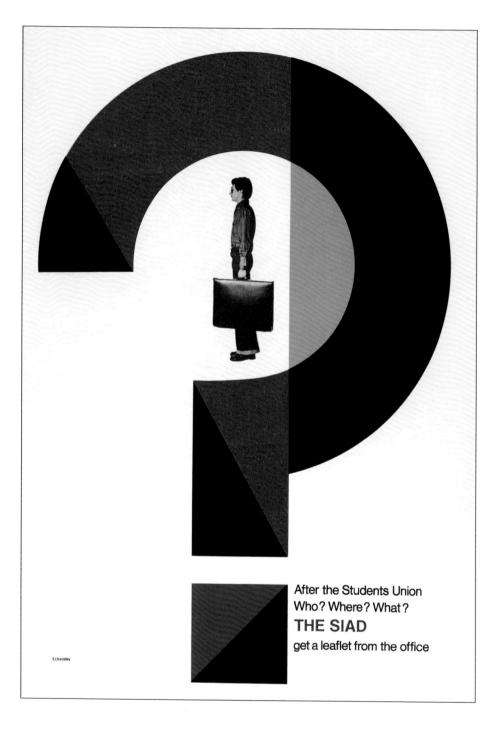

Eckersley

After the Students Union
Who? Where? What?
THE SIAD
get a leaflet from the office

Punctuation
Linguistic signposts

Letters and numbers are not the only great typographic elements. Don't forget punctuation marks. They are not only linguistic aids for reading, they are also abstract signs that often have representational and symbolic weight. You may not be able to tell an entire story using exclamation marks, question marks, commas, dashes and colons, but there is a lot of expression in those marks, as the recent trend in emoticons demonstrates.

Exclamation marks are declarative characters, yet when typeset in an extra bold gothic, one or more exclamation marks will evoke urgency, anxiety or even more demanding emotions. Question marks, while obviously not declarative, are no less demonstrative. Usually a question mark is interrogative and yet, when set large on a layout, it can also be read as a signpost for where answers can be found. The respective meanings of punctuation are limited, but within their individual parameters there is a rich range of typographic possibility.

Tom Eckersley's poster is a perfectly 'geometricized' question mark. Centred as though it is a target, with the bulls-eye in the top half of the character, the mark speaks volumes about the young graduate who is leaving the art-school bubble for the real world. The words 'Who? Where? What?' are used, not in a literal, heavy-handed way, but to complement the dominant question mark.

Typography is the organization of words and yet, sometimes, those words are best conveyed through the shorthand of punctuation. The combination of symbolic and real elements tells a complete story – and, in this case, a startling one at that.

⊠ Tom Eckersley, c. 1990
The Siad

Glossary

Airbrush An electric air-pressure-generated, handheld tool that sprays various media, including paint, ink and dye, originally used for photographic retouching. Today it also describes a digital Photoshop tool to give a spray-painted effect.

Art deco A distinctly 'modern' international art and design movement of the 1920s that began in Europe and spread throughout the industrialized world.

Art nouveau A major turn-of-the-century art and design movement and style, known for its naturalistic ornamentation and excessive use of tendrils and vines.

Baroque A style of European art and design of the seventeenth and eighteenth centuries that fostered ornate detail. Used in modern argot to signify overly decorative graphic design and typography.

Bauhaus The influential state-sponsored German design school (1919 to 1933), closed by the Nazis, known as one of the wellsprings of modern design and typography.

Bézier curve A parametric curve used in computer graphics, running from a start point to an end point, with its curvature influenced by one or more intermediate control points.

Bicameral A bicameral alphabet is one that has two sets of letters.

Byzantine A style of intricately designed art and architecture dating to the Byzantine Empire of the fifth and sixth centuries. Intricate ornamental typography might be referred to as Byzantine.

Constructivism An art and design movement born of the Russian Revolution of 1917, which rejected the idea of art for art's sake in favour of art serving a social purpose. Stylistically known for asymmetrical type compositions, heavy bars, no ornament and limited colour.

Cubist A revolutionary way of creating representations where objects are analysed, broken up and reassembled in an abstracted form. Pioneered by Pablo Picasso and Georges Braque, as a stylistic mannerism it was adopted by graphic designers to express modernity.

Curlicue A fluid form that is rooted in the intersection and intertwining of meandering lines.

Dadaism An anti-art, design and literary movement that began in 1916 in Zurich, Switzerland, and ushered in a revolution of periodical and advertising design. Clashing typefaces, chaotic layouts and raw imagery were its hallmarks.

Dot-screen (see Halftone)

Drop cap Also called 'initial caps', these are enlarged letters used to indicate the beginning of a new chapter, section or paragraph. When ornate they are called illuminated initials.

Fin de siècle Refers to the end of the nineteenth century, particularly the styles of art of that time.

Floppy disk A flexible disk housed in a plastic container used for storing computer data.

Flush Referring to the setting of type straight or justified on left or right or up to a grid line.

Foundry The factory where typefaces were cut and forged. In the digital era, a foundry is a type designer and manufacturer.

Futurism A radical art and design movement founded in Italy in 1909. Futurist typography was know as *parole in libertà* ('words in freedom'), characterized by words composed to represent noise and speech.

Ghosting The trace or remains of a typographic image that was once prominent, yet owing to age or intention, is faded though readable.

Grotesque A subset of gothic or sans serif type that is bold with a wide range of widths used for headlines, advertisements and signs.

Hairline A very thin rule that is made by pen and ink or computer.

Halftone A screen that transforms continuous tone photographs into a pattern of dots to enable printing.

Justified When typography is both flush left and flush right, lined up perfectly on both sides – the opposite of rag right or rag left typesetting.

Kerning Respacing letters or words to achieve pleasing juxtapositions.

Laser-cutting Using a laser to mortise or cut out shapes and patterns in any kind of material.

Letterpress The term associated with vintage printing-apparatus prints copied by direct impression of an inked, raised surface against sheets or a roll of paper.

Ligature Multiple letters that are conjoined into a single character or glyph – a typographic abbreviation.

Litho-crayon A grease pencil or crayon used in lithography that does not absorb ink or liquid. The fat line of a litho-crayon is useful for making bold notations.

Nameplate In newspaper argot this is also the 'masthead', 'word-mark' or name of a publication.

New Typography, The A style of type composition codified by Jan Tschichold in 1928 that broke all the classical rules of form and replaced them with assymmetry, simplicity, sans serifs and limited ornament.

PostScript A computer language for creating vector graphics, particularly in the creation of computer type.

Rebus A puzzle where images are substituted for letters or words in a sentence or phrase.

Retro Referring to the sampling or appropriation of vintage design elements in a contemporary context.

Rococo A style of art that originated in France in the early 1700s and is characterized by elaborate ornamentation, with profusions of scrolls, foliage and animal forms.

Sans-serif Type without **serifs**, or little feet, at the ends of letters.

Silkscreen A printing technique using a mesh to transfer ink onto a substrate, except in areas made impermeable to the ink by a mask.

Slab serif Bold, blocky serifs primarily found in woodtype, but also cut in metal, photo and digital formats.

Slug A piece of metal type from a typesetting machine.

Suprematism A Russian abstract art movement that influenced typography and layout throughout the 1920s. It was rooted on basic geometric forms – circles, squares, lines, and rectangles – painted in a limited range of colours.

Swash A typographical flourish sometimes referred to as a 'tail'.

Swiss typography Also known as the International Style, this is design movement advocated severe limitations on type, colour, picture and ornament, with the goal of legibility, functionality and unfettered readability.

Trompe l'oeil In French the term means 'to fool the eye' and it refers to something created to appear three-dimensional while it is, in fact, only two-dimensional.

Vernacular In typography, 'vernacular' refers to quotidian type or lettering that is used without attention to the finer points of typesetting (e.g. on garage or laundry tickets).

X-Acto knife The brand name of a popular tool used by mechanical artists to cut everything, including type galleys.

Further reading

Baines, Phil and Catherine Dixon. *Signs: Lettering in the Environment*, Laurence King, 2008.

Bataille, Marion. *ABC3D*, Roaring Brook Press, 2008.

Bergström, Bo. *Essentials of Visual Communication*, Laurence King, 2009.

Burke, Christopher. *Active Literature*, Hyphen Press, 2008.

Cabarga, Leslie. *Progressive German Graphics, 1900-1937*. Chronicle Books, 1994.

Carlyle, Paul and Guy Oring. *Letters and Lettering*. McGraw Hill Book Company, Inc., date unknown.

DeNoon, Christopher. *Posters of the WPA 1935–1943*. The Wheatley Press, 1987.

Hayes, Clay. *Gig Posters: Rock Show Art of the 21st Century*, Quirk, 2009.

Heller, Steven. *Merz to Emigre and Beyond: Progressive Magazine Design of the Twentieth Century*. Phaidon Press, 2003.

Heller, Steven and Gail Anderson. *New Vintage Type*, Watson Guptil, 2007.

Heller, Steven and Seymour Chwast. *Graphic Style: From Victorian to Post Modern*, Harry N. Abrams, Inc., 1988.

Heller, Steven and Louise Fili. *Deco Type: Stylish Alphabets of the '20s and '30s*. Chronicle Books, 1997.

------. *Design Connoisseur; An Eclectic Collection of Imagery and Type*, Allworth Press, 2000.

------. *Stylepedia*, Chronicle Books, 2006.

------. *Typology: Type Design from The Victorian Era to The Digital Age*. Chronicle Books, 1999.

Heller, Steven and Mirko Ilic. *Anatomy of Design*, Rockport Publishers, 2007.

------. *Handwritten: Expressive Lettering in the Digital Age*, Thames and Hudson, 2007.

Hollis, Richard. *Graphic Design: A Concise History*, Thames and Hudson, Ltd., 1994.

Kelly, Rob Roy. *American Wood Type 1828–1900: Notes on the Evolution of Decorated and Large Types*. Da Capo Press, Inc., 1969.

Klanten, R. and H. Hellige. *Playful Type: Ephemeral Lettering and Illustrative Fonts*, Die Gestalten Verlag, 2008.

Keith Martin, Robin Dodd, Graham Davis, and Bob Gordon, *1000 Fonts: An Illustrated Guide to Finding the Right Typeface*, Chronicle Books, 2009.

McLean, Ruari. *Jan Tschichold: Typographer*, Lund Humphries, 1975.

------. *Pictorial Alphabets,* Studio Vista, 1969.

Müller, Lars and Victor Malsy. *Helvetica Forever,* Lars Müller Publishers, 2009.

Poynor, Rick. *Typographica,* Princeton Architectural Press, 2002.

Purvis, Alston W. and Martijn F. Le Coultre. *Graphic Design 20th Century,* Princeton Architectural Press, 2003.

Sagmeister, Stefan. *Things I Have Learned in My Life So Far,* Abrams, 2008.

Shaughnessy, Adrian. *How to Be a Graphic Designer without Losing Your Soul,* Laurence King, 2005.

Spencer, Herbert. *Pioneers of Modern Typography,* Hastings House, 1969.

Tholenaar, Jan and Alston W. Purvis, *Type: A Visual History of Typefaces and Graphic Styles,* Vol. 1, Taschen, 2009.

Selected websites

http://fontsinuse.com

http://ilovetypography.com/

http://incredibletypes.com

http://nyctype.co

http://typedia.com

http://typetoy.com

http://typeverything.com

http://typophile.tumblr.com

http://welovetypography.com

http://woodtype.org

www.p22.com

www.ross-macdonald.com

www.typography.com

www.terminaldesign.com

www.typotheque.com

Index

Acknowledgements & Picture credits

We are grateful to the editors, designers and production team at Laurence King Publishing for getting this book off the launch pad.

Specific gratitude goes to senior editor Sophie Wise, commissioning editor Sophie Drysdale, editorial director Jo Lightfoot and, of course, to Laurence King himself.

We are further grateful to all those designers and typographers included in this volume: thank you for allowing us to use your work as exemplars from which others may learn.

Thanks also to Louise Fili, Joe Newton, Lita Talarico, Esther Ro-Schofield, Ron Callahan and Debbie Millman. Finally to David Rhodes, President of the School of Visual Arts (SVA), New York, for his generosity.

Steven Heller and Gail Anderson

11 Original art from Alex Steinweiss Archives **12** Courtesy Andrew Byrom **15** Estate of Saul Bass. All rights reserved/ Paramount Pictures **16** Image courtesy Mehmet Ali Türkmen **19** Images courtesy Dave Towers **21** image courtesy Julie Rutigliano – julierutigliano.com **25** Courtesy Elaine Lustig **26** W* 94/ December 2006 Wallpaper cover by Alan Fletcher. Courtesy of the Alan Fletcher Archive **29** Image courtesy Pentagram **30** Image courtesy Kevin Cantrell/Typography Consulting: Arlo Vance & Spencer Charles **33** Massin/© editions Gallimard **34** The Herb Lubalin Study Center of Design and Typography/ The Cooper Union **37** Agency: OCD | The Original Champions of Design. Design Partners: Jennifer Kinon, Bobby C. Martin Jr. Design: Matt Kay, Jon Lee, Kathleen Fitzgerald. Lettering: Matthew Kay. Design Intern: Desmond Wong **41** Alan Kitching/Baseline **42** Image design © Elvio Gervasi **45** Private collection, London **46** Priest + Grace **49** Courtesy Fiodor Sumkin **50** Burgues Script. Typeface design by Alejandro Paul **53** Courtesy Emigre **57** Jonny Hannah/Heart Agency **58** gray318 **61** © Mouron. Cassandre. Lic. 2015-09-10-01 www.cassandre.fr **62** Seymour Chwast/ Pushpin Group,inc. **65** images courtesy Paul Cox **66** Courtesy Niklaus Troxler **69** Designer: Sascha Hass, Boltz & Hase, Toronto, Canada **70** Image courtesy Ben Barry **75** Courtesy Michiel Schuurman **76** Courtesy of Fshnunlimited magazine, Art Direction & Design by Paul Sych, photography by Mike Ruiz **79** Courtesy Zsuzsanna Ilijin **80** Stephen Doyle/Doyle Partners, New York **85** Private collection, London **86** Courtesy Wim Crouwel **89** Experimental Jetset **90** Image courtesy Wing Lau/www.winglau.net **93** Photograph courtesy of the Museum fur Gestaltung, Zurich, Poster collection **94** Photograph courtesy of the Museum fur Gestaltung, Zurich, Poster collection/ DACS 2015 **97** Courtesy Aron Jancso **101** Photo by Brian Cooke/Redferns/ Getty Images. Jamie Reid courtesy John Marchant Gallery. Copyright Sex Pistols Residuals **105** "I Love NY" logo used with permission by the New York State Department of Economic Development **106** Image courtesy Rizon Parein **110** Title: A for Annual Year: 2006. Designer: Paul Belford. Client: Creative Review Magazine **113** Series of Posters for the Moscow International Typography Festival Typomania (2015 www. typomania.ru/Art Director and Designer Alexander Vasin, Photographer, Boris Bendikov **115** The Lester Beall Collection, Cary Graphic Arts Collection, Rochester Institute of Technology **116** Courtesy Brody Associates **119** Private collection, London **120** with thanks to the Tom Eckersley Estate and the University of the Arts London